COPING™

COPING WITH DEPRESSION

Avery Elizabeth Hurt

Rosen YA™
New York

Published in 2020 by The Rosen Publishing Group, Inc.
29 East 21st Street, New York, NY 10010

First Edition

Library of Congress Cataloging-in-Publication Data

Names: Hurt, Avery Elizabeth, author.
Title: Coping with depression / Avery Elizabeth Hurt.
Description: First edition. | New York : Rosen Publishing, 2020. | Series: Coping | Includes bibliographical references and index. | Audience: Grades 7–12.
Identifiers: LCCN 2018060310| ISBN 9781508187288 (library bound) | ISBN 9781508187271 (paperback)
Subjects: LCSH: Depression in adolescence—Juvenile literature.
Classification: LCC RJ506.D4 H87 2020 | DDC 616.85/2700835—dc23
LC record available at https://lccn.loc.gov/2018060310

Manufactured in the United States of America

For many of the images in this book, the people photographed are models. The depictions do not imply actual situations or events.

CONTENTS

INTRODUCTION

You've probably heard more than one well-meaning adult say something like, "These are the best years of your life!" To you, it may sound like they have no recollection whatsoever of what it was like to be a teen. You're trying to get grades that will get you into a decent college so you can prepare for a good career. But you have no idea what you want to do next week, much less for the rest of your life. Of course, good grades aren't enough. You also have to take part in extracurricular activities and do community work—as if you could find the time for that. It seems like you never get enough sleep.

Meanwhile, your friends are acting weird, and you're not sure where your relationship stands anymore. That person you have a crush on just broke your heart—and worse than that, everybody in your class knows about it. Social media is a landmine. If you say something dumb, it will be all over school by morning. If you don't join in, you'll have zero friends. And some jerk in tenth grade posted mean things about you on Snapchat.

It seems like it's getting harder and harder to get along with your parents. They expect you to act like

Schoolwork and organized activities can often extend into evenings and weekends. That decrease in downtime can increase stress and the feeling of being overwhelmed.

an adult, but they still treat you like a child. Your brothers and sisters are driving you up a wall. Your body doesn't help, either. Your hormones are all over the place and your face has become the official home for lost acne.

Adolescence is difficult for almost everybody, but most people get through it just fine. Then they grow up to become those adults who are always going on about how wonderful the teens years are.

Some people, however, experience something much worse than typical teenage angst. According to the National Institute of Mental Health (NIMH), about one in five teens will experience depression before they become adults.

In today's busy world, getting enough quality sleep is harder than ever. But it's important to get rest. Lack of sleep is one of the risk factors for depression.

Depression can be relatively mild and short lived, or it can be ongoing and life-threatening. Whatever form depression takes, it is serious. Depression can lead to suicide, which, according to the Centers for Disease Control and Prevention (CDC), is the second-leading cause of death in people ages fifteen to nineteen.

Health care professionals have a wealth of therapies and techniques for treating depression. This makes the outlook for people with depression more hopeful than it has ever been.

All this sounds pretty dismal, but actually there is some very good news about depression. In recent years, scientists have learned a great deal about the illness. They've been able to dismiss a lot of stereotypes and myths. They've demonstrated that depression is a biological illness, not just moodiness or an inability to cope. They've also found many new and effective ways to treat depression. In the coming pages, you will learn what depression is, whom it affects, and what you can do if you or someone you love suffers from this all-too-common illness.

CHAPTER ONE

What Depression Is—and What It's Not

People often say things like, "That was a depressing movie," or, "All these rainy days have made me depressed," or "The new school uniforms are so depressing." But these feelings aren't really depression—at least not the kind of depression that is the focus of this book. So, what is depression? It might be easier to start by talking about what it is not.

Not Just Sadness

When people think of depression, they often think of sadness. Sadness can be a part of depression, but it's not the only or even the primary symptom of the illness. A person can

Clinical depression is far more than just the rainy-day blues. However, feeling sad—especially for no reason—and not getting over it quickly can be a sign of depression.

be very sad, but not depressed. It's perfectly normal—and not a sign of illness—to feel sad when something bad happens. Failing a big test or having a fight with parents or a friend can make a person feel sad. If a beloved pet dies or a best friend moves away, almost anyone would feel sad. This is not depression. It's just a normal reaction to a life event.

Sometimes people think that depression is just a kind of moodiness—sort of like being out of sorts or in a snit. But that's not what depression is either. Depression is one of a group of illnesses called mood disorders, but it is far more than just being moody. When people are depressed, they might feel all kinds of emotions, including anger, irritability, and, yes, sadness. Or they may have trouble feeling any emotions. People who suffer from depression often say that the worst part of the illness is that they feel empty and can't seem to care about anything at all. Depression can cause people to have trouble sleeping. Or it can make them just want to sleep all the time. People with depression can lose their appetites. Or they might overeat. They can have trouble paying attention or completing tasks. They can feel scatterbrained and have memory problems. But these are just symptoms of depression, not the disease itself.

All these different feelings can make it hard to understand exactly what depression is. But one thing is clear, depression is not a normal reaction to life. It is not just moodiness, sadness, or "the blues." It is an illness. Difficulties and stresses in life can contribute to depression; sometimes they can even trigger an episode of depression. But the illness itself is a disorder of the brain. Depression is a medical condition. And it is one that can be treated.

Why Me?

Depression is a serious problem among all ages and all types of people. According to the National Institute of Mental Health, in the United States, women are far more likely to suffer from depression than men, and teenage girls are slightly more likely to suffer from depression than men and teenage boys. (Among children, before puberty, girls and boys seem to have roughly the same rates of depression.) But don't be fooled. Guys of all ages get depression, too. The CDC also points out that people who live in poverty are more likely to be depressed than people who are more financially secure. But no matter what their social or racial background, anyone can get depression. And according to data gathered by the National Alliance on Mental Illness (NAMI), one of the times in life when you are at the greatest risk of depression is during adolescence.

Scientists aren't totally sure why the teenage years are an especially risky time for depression, but they have a few clues. During adolescence, the body goes through a lot of chemical changes. Sex hormones and growth hormones are flooding the brain. This can have some strange effects on the mind. (This also may be one reason that women are at higher risk for depression during the years just before menopause. That's when the brain undergoes the biggest hormonal realignment since adolescence.)

It's a Guy Thing, Too

Rates of depression are slightly higher for teen girls than boys, though not by much. But boys can have one other problem that girls don't. They live in a culture that often discourages men and boys from admitting problems and asking for help, especially when those problems are emotional. Though the perception is changing, many people still believe that men should rarely show emotion and never admit to weakness. This is utter nonsense and is

one of the most destructive stigmas surrounding mental illness. Sadly, though, a lot of people—even guys with depression—believe it. That keeps them from reaching out for help when they need it. A young woman might feel comfortable telling a friend she may be depressed. A young man might be completely unwilling to take the risk that his friend will think he's weak or less manly for having emotional problems.

(continued on the next page)

Guys get depression, too, though they are far less likely to recognize and admit it. That means they often don't get the care that is available.

(continued from the previous page)

Fortunately, guys are starting to realize that having depression doesn't make them weak, it makes them human. When that happens, they can give themselves and their friends who have depression the kind of care and support they need. There's another advantage to getting rid of the "guys are tough" notion. When guys can explore and express their own emotions, they are much better prepared to have deep and lasting relationships with others, including friends, family members, and romantic partners.

What Does It Do?

You don't need a scientist to tell you that depression can seriously mess with your life. Besides making you miserable, depression can make it difficult to concentrate and pay attention. That makes it hard to keep up in school. Depressed people tend to be unreliable. They might not keep their promises or show up when they said they would. They might say things they don't mean or snap at people. This kind of behavior is tough on relationships with teachers, friends, and family. It makes it difficult to make new friends, too. Depressed people don't always behave in these ways, but often they do.

Often depressed people use alcohol or drugs to help them feel better or to get their minds off their troubles. Sadly, this just creates even more problems. It can also make depression worse because alcohol and many drugs can contribute to depression.

Of course, the very worst consequence of depression is suicide. According to the National Institute of Mental Health, more than forty thousand Americans die by suicide each year. In Canada, that number is around four thousand people, according to Statistics Canada. In the past decade or so, suicide rates among teens have risen in both nations.

Depression in the Halls of Power

You might think that having depression would limit a person's chances for doing great things—like leading the world, for example. Nope.

(continued on the next page)

(continued from the previous page)

Researchers at Duke University Medical Center took a close look at biographical sources of US presidents. They found that at least half of those who served from 1776 to 1974 had some form of mental illness. Twenty-four percent had depression. Others suffered from anxiety.

Abraham Lincoln is well known for suffering intense depression during the Civil War. (That's really not too surprising. The Civil War probably made a lot of people depressed.) James Madison, John Quincy Adams, Franklin Pierce, and Calvin Coolidge also had depression, according to the Duke study. In addition, the study's authors think that Thomas Jefferson, Ulysses S. Grant, and Woodrow Wilson suffered from anxiety and that Lyndon Johnson and Theodore Roosevelt may have suffered from bipolar disorder (a kind of depression that alternates depressive phases with manic phases).

In case you think it has something to do with being president of the United States, know that it's not just US leaders. Winston Churchill, who was prime minister of Britain during World War II, suffered terribly from depression. He called depression his "black dog." Mahatma Gandhi, the

Abraham Lincoln (*left*) and Winston Churchill (*right*) battled depression. Lincoln was a much-admired US president, and Churchill helped lead Britain and the Allies to victory during World War II.

man who lead India to independence from Britain, also struggled with depression.

Some notable leaders in business, science, and the arts may have had depression, too. Charles Dickens, Georgia O'Keeffe, and Isaac Newton make this list.

The Essential Horror

All these consequences of depression are bad. But what people who aren't depressed often don't realize is just how awful depression *feels* to people who suffer from it. Some people romanticize depression, calling it a "beautiful sadness," or identifying it with poets or rock stars who have been depressed. But anyone who has actually been depressed can tell you that there's nothing beautiful about it. In a 2000 interview, J. K. Rowling, author of the Harry Potter books, told Ann Treneman, a journalist for *The Times of London*, that she had experienced depression. Rowling described depression like this, "It is that absence of being able to envisage that you will ever be cheerful again. The absence of hope. That very deadened feeling, which is so very different from feeling sad. Sad hurts but it's a healthy feeling. It's a necessary thing to feel. Depression is very different." In a short story called "The Depressed Person," David Foster Wallace, who suffered from depression and eventually died by suicide, once described depression as an "essential horror" that entails

J. K. Rowling has said that her experience with depression helped her to create the Dementors that appear in the Harry Potter books.

"terrible and unceasing emotional pain." It is, he wrote, "an indescribable hell on earth." Depression can be difficult to describe, but one thing people who have dealt with it agree on: it's not beautiful.

Perhaps it is because it's so hard for those who suffer from depression to explain what they are going through that there are so many misconceptions and stigmas about the illness. Because people don't understand depression, it can be frightening or make them uncomfortable. Despite efforts to educate the public about depression, some people still think that people get depressed because they are weak and don't know how to cope with life. They think that being depressed is somehow the fault of the person with the illness. When people find out their friends have depression, they may not know how to respond. They may try to avoid that person or make tasteless jokes. Or maybe they try to be kind but end up saying the wrong things.

This can cause people who have depression to be ashamed and want to hide their illness. Obviously, that makes it much harder for them to get the help they need. If people are afraid that they will be criticized or condemned for having depression, they aren't likely to admit it to their friends and parents. Sometimes they don't admit it even to themselves. The only way to make this better is to educate people about depression. If they know what it is, they will recognize myths and stigmas when they see them.

It's important to keep in mind that depression is something you *have*, not who you are. Depression isn't something that defines a person. Having depression does not mean a person is weak, defective, or a loser. It simply means that that person has an illness and needs medical help.

Fortunately, attitudes about depression (and other mental illnesses) are changing. People are learning what depression is—and isn't—and that makes it easier for them to relate to friends with depression. And it makes it easier for people who have depression to speak up and ask for help. And asking for help is even more important than it used to be. Why? Because today there is a great deal of help available for people with depression.

Myths & FACTS

Myth: Depression is something you can pull yourself out of.

Fact: You may be able to do that with bad moods and ordinary blues. But depression is a much more formidable adversary. It takes professional help to deal with depression. People aren't expected to pull themselves out of other illnesses, like diabetes. They shouldn't be expected to do that with depression.

Myth: If someone is able to go to school and take part in other activities, the depression must not be too bad.

Fact: Depression can be debilitating. But the effects of depression aren't always so obvious. Just because a person seems OK doesn't mean he or she is. And being able to function is never a reason to forgo reaching out for help.

Myth: Admitting you have depression to people is admitting you're a failure.

Fact: This is just plain wrong. It can't be said enough: depression is an illness. Some people get it, others don't. Whether or not a person has depression has absolutely nothing to do with his or her strength of character or value as a person.

CHAPTER TWO

A Scientific Matter

Depression can seem like a condition of modern life. But it's not a new illness. In the fifth century BCE, the Greek physician Hippocrates discussed depression. He called it "melancholia," but clearly he was talking about what today we call depression. The symptoms he described are the same ones people with depression experience today. Hippocrates was the first person we know of to realize that depression was a physical illness. However, it took another couple of centuries

Hippocrates, widely known today for the Hippocratic oath that physicians take before beginning to practice, is often called the father of medicine. He wrote about depression.

before scientists began to understand the biological roots of depression, and doctors learned how to treat it effectively.

Family Ties and the Tangles of Life

The causes of depression are extremely complex. Depression is sometimes referred to as a chemical imbalance of the brain. But that may be too simple a way to explain it. The fact is, there are many chemicals involved in helping regulate mood. And they can get out of whack in a variety of different ways. One brain chemical that seems to be involved in depression is called serotonin. Serotonin helps different regions of the brain communicate with one another and is especially involved in processing emotions. Scientists have discovered that people who have depression often have fewer receptors for serotonin. This means that even if they have plenty of serotonin in their bodies, their brains can't use it effectively.

People with depression often have too much of a brain chemical called cortisol. Cortisol is a stress hormone. Scientists think that it may damage parts of the brain that process emotion. There are many more brain chemicals involved in depression, and not all are well understood. But as scientists work to understand the disease, they are learning more about these chemicals. They are also learning about the many things that can affect how these chemicals work. They still have a lot to learn. One thing is sure, though. Depression is the result of an interaction between many different factors.

Heredity is one factor. People who have a family history of depression are more likely to get depression than people who don't. This has been shown in several studies, including one published in 2016 in a publication of the *Journal of the American Medical Association.* Certain life experiences can set off a bout of depression in people who have the biological tendency to get the illness. Grief and sadness are not themselves depression, but they can trigger it in some people. Physical, sexual, or emotional abuse can cause depression. Social problems, such as being bullied or isolated at school, are very likely to cause depression. Major life events can, too. Moving,

A family history of depression can increase an individual's risk of the disease. Family ties can also make it easier to cope if depression strikes.

changing schools, going to college, or a divorce in the family can all potentially trigger depression. The events don't even have to be negative—they just have to be big deals. Stress at school, certain medications, and chronic illnesses can also cause depression.

We say these things cause depression, but as we know, the causes are very complex. No single thing causes depression. Brain chemistry, life events, and heredity all work together. If things fall just the right way (or really, it's the wrong way), you might get depression. But even if you check all these boxes, you won't necessarily get depression.

Labeling Depression

People often talk about depression as if it's just one disease. But actually there are several forms of depression.

Major depressive disorder: This is a deep depression that one experiences at least two days a week and lasts two weeks or longer.

Persistent depressive disorder: This is when the depression lasts two years or longer.

Bipolar disorder: This type of illness can be very different from major and persistent depressive disorder. People who suffer from bipolar disorder often swing dramatically from periods of mania to periods of depression. During the manic periods, they can be extremely active and talkative. They might take on huge projects or take risks they

(continued on the next page)

(continued from the previous page)

wouldn't normally take. During the depressive phase, they have much less energy and experience the symptoms usually associated with major depression. People sometimes describe manic phases as the "up" or "happy" phase of the disorder. But, in fact, it is characterized by activity and energy, not necessarily happiness. People going through a manic phase can sometimes be very aggressive as well.

Seasonal affective disorder: This is fittingly abbreviated as SAD. This kind of depression is common during winter, when there is not much sun. Light therapy can help with SAD.

Postpartum depression: New mothers can experience this type of depression right after the birth of a child. It is thought to be caused by hormonal disturbances.

Brain in Motion

Until the 1980s, experts didn't think young people could get depression. They thought that since young brains were still maturing, that would keep them from getting depression. Now, of course, they realize that young people are at great risk for the illness. One of the reasons they're at such risk is *because* their brains are maturing. Adolescence is a difficult time for a young brain.

You may have noticed—or your parents may have pointed out—that your moods are all over the place these days. One minute you're feeling sweet and easygoing. The next minute you're snapping people's heads off. Some days you can't get enough of your friends. Other days you just want to hang out in your room reading or listening to music. You may find it hard to make decisions. Or you make decisions without thinking about the consequences. This emotional chaos is perfectly normal for teenagers. But why is it normal?

Part of it, of course, is hormones. Sex hormones, growth hormones, and stress hormones are produced in great quantities during the teen years. But hormones aren't the only part of the picture. In fact, during adolescence, the brain is totally rewiring itself. It prunes a lot of the connections between nerve cells that it made during childhood.

It makes new connections in different parts of the brain. Some of these connections aren't finalized until the early twenties. And the parts of the brain where emotions are regulated are among the last to finalize these new connections.

None of this causes depression. If it did, all teens would be depressed. But it does explain why mental health can be a bit fragile during the teen years. Understanding what's going on in the teen brain can also help scientists come up with ways to treat these problems. In recent years, there has been a lot of progress in treating teen depression.

The Science of Deduction

The first step to getting help, of course, is seeing a doctor. Many people are reluctant to do that. Some think that the problem will go away or that they can deal with it themselves. Others know they need professional help but are ashamed to ask for it.

Of those who do go to the doctor, many don't actually get the help that is available. Depression can be tricky to diagnose. There isn't a blood test

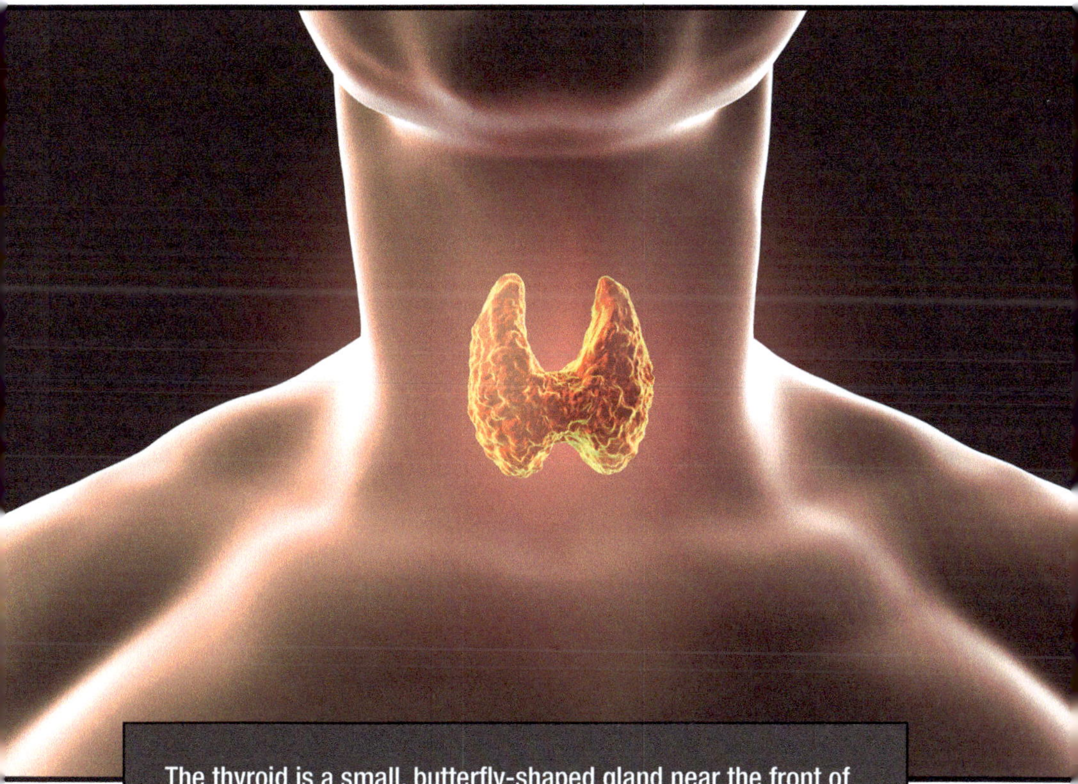

The thyroid is a small, butterfly-shaped gland near the front of the neck. It produces chemicals that regulate metabolism. When it's not doing its job properly, the result can be depression.

to confirm it. You can't see depression on an X-ray or CT scan. However, doctors do have ways of determining if a patient has depression. The doctor will check to make sure there isn't anything else wrong that can be causing the symptoms. (Like thyroid problems, for example.) Then she'll ask a lot of questions about how the person has been feeling lately. She'll ask questions like:

- Do you feel sad or in a depressed mood every day or most days?
- Do you no longer enjoy things you used to enjoy?
- Have you lost or gained a lot of weight recently? Has your appetite changed?
- Do you have trouble sleeping or do you sleep much more than you used to?
- Do you feel tired all the time or do you tire easily?
- Do you have trouble concentrating or making decisions?
- Do you often feel edgy or irritable?
- Do you feel hopeless? Worthless? Do you feel a lot of guilt?
- Do you think about death a lot? Have you thought about, planned, or attempted suicide?

These questions are all about symptoms of depression. No single item on this list means a person has depression, and some can be symptoms of other illnesses as well. But if someone has experienced several of the items on this list more than just occasionally, the doctor will likely consider the possibility that he or she has depression. In addition, the doctor will pay close attention to the patient's general attitude and appearance. She will also ask about a family history of depression. Doctors are a bit like the fictional detective Sherlock Holmes. They look at all the clues and all the evidence and deduce what's going on.

Talk It Over

Once a doctor has made a diagnosis of depression, the next step is determining the best treatment. Fortunately, these days there are many effective medical treatments for depression. Treatments generally fall into one of two types: talk therapy and medication. For many people, a combination of talk therapy and medication is most helpful.

Talk therapy is also called psychotherapy or counseling. In talk therapy, patients meet regularly to talk with a psychologist or other counselor. These meetings are called sessions. They may go alone or they may go with their family. Usually there will be a combination of one-on-one sessions and family sessions. The goal of this therapy is to help patients figure out why they are depressed and help them feel happier and more in control of their lives and feelings. A therapist will help patients find ways to improve their relationships and deal with their problems.

There are several approaches to talk therapy. One that has been very effective in treating depression is called cognitive behavioral therapy (CBT). Cognitive therapy focuses on how a person thinks, feels, and behaves now. It doesn't spend much time on early childhood experiences or traumas that may have contributed to depression. Instead, it helps patients change the way they think about themselves and their experiences. It is very practical and offers many useful tools for dealing with the issues that come up in life.

Interpersonal psychological therapy (IPT) is another kind of talk therapy that has been helpful for young people with depression. Unlike cognitive therapy, interpersonal therapy focuses on the external events and relationships that are going on in the patient's life.

There are other approaches to psychotherapy. Doctors help patients and their families decide which is best for them.

A Prescription for Wellness

We're always hearing warnings about how dangerous drugs can be. And that's fair. But prescribed medicines can sometimes be lifesavers. This is no less true of depression medicines than of medicines like insulin for people with diabetes. Several medicines have been approved for teens with depression. It can sometimes take a few attempts to figure out which medicine is best and which dose is ideal. It's super important to take the medicine exactly as the doctor says.

Depression medicines can sometimes cause a few unpleasant side effects, such as stomach problems, insomnia, and weight gain. These symptoms usually go away after the body gets used to the drug. When patients have problems taking the medicine, though, they mustn't just stop taking it. That can cause more problems. It's best to let a doctor help decide what to do.

According to an article by Dr. Steven Cuffe on the website of the American Academy of Child and Adolescent Psychiatry, there has been some evidence that a few of the more common depression medicines

If you or someone you know is suicidal, don't wait. Immediately seek help. If no adult is near, call the Suicide Prevention Hotline. Someone is always available to help, twenty-four hours a day.

can actually increase the risk of suicide. Of course, being depressed is the biggest risk for suicide. According to Dr. Cuffe and others, caution is warranted. However, these medicines are still valuable when used carefully. The important thing for people who take these medicines to remember is to keep their parents and doctors informed about how they're feeling and to let someone know immediately if they begin to feel worse or think about suicide.

CHAPTER THREE

Signs of the Times

Depression is not a new illness. But it does seem to be getting more common in recent years—especially among teens. In 2018, in a report called "Major Depression: the Impact on Overall Health," the insurance company Blue Cross/Blue Shield reported some disturbing findings. Since 2013, diagnoses of major depression have increased by 47 percent for male teens and 65 percent for female teens. No one knows exactly why, but modern life offers a lot of clues.

Media, Social, and Other Problems

Today's teens face stresses and insecurities that were unknown a decade ago: school shootings, terrorist attacks, and a proliferation of hate crimes. Their parents' jobs don't seem secure, and they never know when the next economic crisis will hit.

Taking some time away from the noise and bustle is good for everybody once in a while. That's harder to do now, though, because it's so easy to stay connected.

They're not sure there'll be a job for them when they need one. Colleges are more competitive, and a degree is no guarantee of a job even if you make it through and graduate. Climate change is getting worse, and no one seems to be doing much about it. Bullies now have the internet to make their sadism even more effective.

On top of all this, there's the hyperconnectivity of today's world. In the past, kids could get away from everything now and then. But these days, everyone is only a text or a Snapchat post away from everyone else. People feel that they have to be "on" all the time. Yet while they're "on," there's always the risk of embarrassing themselves, offending someone, or otherwise screwing up in front of basically the entire world. The pressure is intense and very nearly constant.

Social media poses other problems as well. It can be hard to live up to other people's standards. It's all too easy for people to compare their lives with the lives of people they see online—and feel that they come up short. Everyone knows that these posts are highly curated. People don't show their awful selfies and broadcast their failures. Even so, other people's posts can be intimidating.

Bullies on Steroids

Bullies are nothing new. They've probably been around ever since humans developed the ability to speak, giving them a handy way to call each other mean names. Literature is full of bullies—from William Shakespeare's Iago in the play *Othello* to Draco Malfoy in the Harry Potter books. But today's bullies have tools that would have made Iago drool with envy. Not that long ago, bullies could menace their victims only in person. If someone were being tormented by a bully at school, he could at least get away from the bully at the end of the day. Even during the school day, the only people who witnessed the humiliation were those who happened to be around when it took place. All that changed the day the world stepped into the internet age.

Thanks to the internet and social media, bullies can now follow their victims wherever they go. People who've been targeted by a bully can feel like the bully is living in their pockets. And the audience for the cruelty is virtually unlimited.

Bullying by means of the internet is called cyberbullying. The US government's antibullying website, stopbullying.gov, describes cyberbullying like this:

Smartphones help us stay in touch with friends and families. Sadly, they also help bullies stay in touch with their victims—and give them a wider audience for their abuse.

Cyberbullying can occur through SMS, Text, and apps, or online in social media, forums, or gaming where people can view, participate in, or share content. Cyberbullying includes sending, posting, or sharing negative, harmful, false, or mean content about someone else. It can include sharing personal or private information about someone else causing embarrassment or humiliation. Some

(continued on the next page)

(continued from the previous page)

cyberbullying crosses the line into unlawful or criminal behavior.

Fortunately, there has been a great deal of awareness of the problem in recent years. If you or someone you know is being bullied in person or online, tell a teacher or your school principal. He or she wants to help, and increasingly school staff are getting training in the best way to provide that help.

Is This the Best Adults Can Do?

The national and international political situation isn't helping, either. It's difficult to get away from the news. That can mean a daily, if not hourly, dose of drama and outrage. Teens often want to get involved and try to do something about the world's problems. They might like to speak out about issues that matter to them, maybe climate change or gun reform, or even a local issue, like more funding for schools or city parks. But then they see that kids who do get involved are being subjected to extreme harassment and bullying—often by adults and even national leaders.

No matter where on the political spectrum you fall—or even if you couldn't care less about policy and politics— it's hard not to be buffeted by the political winds. Traditional media's preference for alarming news makes it difficult to find reasons to be hopeful. Social media's preference for short, witty commentary rather than thoughtful, well-reasoned debate only makes the situation worse.

Depressed teens say they often feel hopeless. It's not hard to see why.

The Upside

Loneliness and isolation are hallmarks of depression. The internet and social media can add to those feelings if we spend too much time in virtual relationships and not enough in real ones. Let's face it; it can be difficult to have a deep, satisfying conversation by text. And it can be impossible to have that kind of talk in person when everyone keeps stopping to check their phones. But don't trash your smartphone yet! (As if you would even consider that!) For all its problems, social media and increased connectivity can be a good thing. They can even help with depression.

The internet and social media make it possible to stay in touch with friends and family who are far away. In the past, if your best friend moved to another city, it would be very difficult to maintain the friendship. Today, you can do that easily using FaceTime or similar apps. Not that long ago, it was hard for kids to get in touch with their parents when they were at work, especially if they wanted to have a private chat. Now most parents are accessible by email or text throughout the day.

Relationships with older people can be enormously beneficial to young people. Teens often find that their grandparents, or other older friends and family members, are delighted to hear from them now and then, maybe via email or even a phone call. They can be a great source of support. They might have lived in a very different world from the one their grandkids are now navigating. Still, they have had experiences that younger people could never dream about. Their experiences and insights might be very useful.

The internet allows people who don't fit in well at school or in their neighborhoods to make friends in other places. There are many online support groups for people with various problems. Therapists can help their patients find a support group that suits them. The internet is loaded with information about depression. There's a lot of misinformation out there, and some bad actors who might take advantage of innocent kids. But with the help of parents, guidance counselors, and doctors, teens should be able to find plenty of helpful material. (Here's a tip: seek out websites of reputable organizations, such as the American Psychological Association or the American Academy of Pediatrics. Also check out university or medical center websites. And remember, just having "Dr." before their names doesn't make people experts.)

Sorry, I Can't Come to the Phone Right Now

To make modern technology work for you, rather than against you, you have to know how to use it wisely and well. And using it wisely can mean turning it off sometimes. A 2018 survey by Pew Research found that more than half of teens think they spend too much time online or on their phones. Sixty percent think that phone time is a "major problem." You read that right. More than half of teens said that, not their parents or teachers. So if teens feel that way, why aren't they turning off their phones?

Everyone knows that disconnecting is easier said than done. Checking messages and social media feeds every few minutes can become a deeply ingrained

Some places—like parts of hospitals or construction sites—restrict cell phone use. Setting your own "no phones" spaces and times can be a good idea.

habit. People do it without even thinking about it. In an article in *Science in the News,* a Harvard University blog, Trevor Haynes, a research technician in the neurobiology department at Harvard Medical School, explains that scientists have discovered that people get a little rush of pleasure when their phones ding to let them know they have a message. We may not be totally aware of it, but our brains are. It's very much like an addiction. Fortunately, it's not as hard to break as a drug addiction. Just cutting back and setting some ground rules can put the control back in your hands.

Completely give up phone time probably wouldn't be a good idea even if you could pull it off. But cutting back here and there can be a huge relief. For example, some people shut down their phones an hour or so before bed. Don't worry. Those messages will still be there in the morning. It's hard at first, but once they're used to having a little alone time at night, some people find that they want to at least get some breakfast in them and prepare for the day before checking in again.

Now they're ready to take it to the next level. They turn their phones to silent or leave them in their rooms during meals. If their parents keep checking their phones during dinner, they challenge them to disconnect for that time, too. Going phone free is a good idea any time you're having a conversation with a living, breathing person. It shows that person the courtesy of paying attention to what he or she is saying. The internet will still be there when the

Spending time outside, reading books (not just blogs!), drawing, and just enjoying your own company—all of these are ways to recharge and improve your mental health.

conversation is over. A lot of people also like to set aside a couple of blocks of time each day—say thirty minutes—just for themselves. That's private time, and no one can intrude by phone. It's a way to do something nice for oneself. It's also a way to make it clear that *you,* not the rest of the world, are in charge of how you spend your time and what you do with your thoughts.

Cutting back on phone and social media use, even just a bit, causes something weird to happen. We realize how nice it is to live life in person rather than through a screen. Screens are good—even necessary—but they aren't everything. It can be very nice to spend a little time in the real world.

So what do people do when they're not on their phones? If they're smart, they go outside. Researchers at Stanford University found that spending time in nature, even if it's just the backyard or a nearby park, reduces the risk of depression. Physical activity is also extremely helpful for mood disorders. Go for a bike ride, shoot a few baskets, or just take a walk.

Encourage Others

There is a story in the Buddhist tradition. A student comes to the teacher who is training him. The student says, "Master, I am discouraged. What should I do?' The master replies, "Encourage others." It's truly amazing how much it can help someone to help others. When feeling down, a little overwhelmed about life or the state of the world, it can work wonders to reach out to others and do just one small thing. There are plenty of opportunities in the community or at school to do volunteer work. Some people help younger kids with their homework. Others drop by and chat with lonely seniors. Something as simple and easy as walking around the park, picking up garbage, and putting it in the bins can do a world of good. It doesn't have to be much to make a huge difference in the world and in your own mind and heart.

CHAPTER FOUR

See It, Know It, Help It

After reading about depression as described by J. K. Rowling and David Foster Wallace, it might seem like the illness would be hard to miss. But actually, it's not always easy to recognize depression in oneself or one's friends.

Not Always What You Expect

The teenage brain has a lot to deal with. Even normal adolescence is a turbulent time. Depression can get lost in the chaos. In an adult, the typical signs of depression—such as sleep problems, irritability, changes in appetite—stand out. In a teen, those things can seem like part of the ups and downs of adolescence. That's why it's important for teens to be aware of the signs of depression, particularly the

Because the symptoms can often be deceiving, it's important to learn all the signs of depression in oneself—and in one's friends and family.

more subtle signs. Feeling extremely sad without any reason or feeling hopeless are definitely indications of depression. Other common signs are pessimism and suicidal thoughts.

However, some indications that a person might be depressed are a little harder to recognize. They don't always look like depression on the surface. Even the person who is depressed might not realize that's what's going on. Here are some of the more subtle signs of depression:

- **Lost focus:** Memory problems and trouble concentrating are classic symptoms of depression. But they don't really scream "depression" to most people. When depression shows up in this way, it's easy to misdiagnose it as attention-deficit/hyperactivity disorder (ADHD). It's even more difficult in a person who also has ADHD. These symptoms can also seem like a normal response to the craziness of life. If a person is having trouble focusing, a doctor will check to see if the problem is ADHD. But she will also screen for depression.

- **Physical pain:** Unexplained aches and pains—backaches, headaches, stomachaches—that come and go without any obvious cause can sometimes indicate depression. If no other illnesses appear to be causing these problems, depression may be the culprit.
- **Fatigue:** In the busy life of a typical teen, being tired seems normal. But feeling tired even when you haven't been all that busy can be a sign of depression. Also, feeling tired even after having slept or rested can be a warning sign.
- **Substance abuse:** People with depression often drink too much or take drugs to help ease the emotional pain. It can make them feel better temporarily, but it actually makes the depression worse.
- **Anger:** Sometimes people with depression get into arguments or even fights over small things. They might escalate a minor disagreement into something major. This may be a way to deal with the emotional numbness that so often characterizes depression. To people with depression,

feeling angry may be better than feeling nothing at all.

- **Perfectionism:** An excessive desire to be perfect in school, appearance, or sports can be a sign of depression. People with depression are often afraid of making mistakes. They also can have low self-esteem. Trying too hard to succeed may be a way of coping with that.
- **Guilt:** Feelings of guilt often accompany depression. Sometimes people with depression spend a lot of time focusing on actions in their past that they regret. They can dwell on past failures. Often these are not things a healthy person would feel bad about, such as having been a mischievous toddler. Often depressed people even feel guilty about being depressed!
- **Inability to accept praise:** Not being able to accept compliments or routine kindness can be a sign of depression. So is not feeling worthy of awards or honors one has obviously earned.
- **Excessive socializing:** Spending time with family and friends is healthy. It can often help relieve depression. But sometimes people

with depression go overboard. They spend too much time socializing and can't stand to be alone.

None of these things means a person definitely has depression. Many of them can be perfectly normal, such as being tired or going to a lot of parties. Some, such as headaches or backaches, are signs of other illnesses. But all of these can be easy-to-miss signs of depression. It can be tricky to know when these things are signs of depression and when they're normal. Two indications that depression may be behind these symptoms are when any of these symptoms are extreme, and when one or more of these symptoms pop up in several areas of life. For example, say someone can't seem to concentrate in band but is doing fine in algebra. That may just mean she's tired of the clarinet but really into quadratic equations. But if a formerly engaged student just can't focus on any classes, it's worth checking to see if depression may be the problem.

Psychotherapy, or talk therapy, is a proven treatment for depression. It can also help with other mental illnesses, such as anxiety or bipolar disorder.

Reach Out

Depression is an illness. Often a very serious illness. But it can be treated. There is no need for anyone to suffer alone with depression. However, it's not always easy for teens with depression to seek help.

Teens often worry that they're overreacting. What if they tell someone they're depressed, and it turns out to be nothing? They've made a big deal of nothing and called attention to themselves. Maybe they've cost their parents money for doctor's appointments and missed work. However, if someone even thinks that he or she *might* be depressed, it's important to check it out. That may mean he or she has caught the illness in the early stages when it's much easier to treat.

Sometimes people know they need help, but they don't want to worry their parents. This is a bigger problem for kids who are the most seriously depressed. They know it's a big deal. They just don't want their parents to have to cope with it. Of course, their parents want to know so that they can get help as soon as possible. They would much rather have to deal with a depressed child than lose the child to suicide. Also, depressed people don't always realize how many difficulties their illnesses cause others. Their parents are probably already worried. They might be relieved to be asked to help.

Teens who don't have good relationships with their parents often keep their troubles to themselves. This may seem brave. But it's not. It's incredibly dangerous. Teens who are struggling with emotions need to talk to a trusted adult. No one should try to deal with mental illness alone. When parents aren't an option, there are others to reach out to. Teens can talk to a trusted teacher, guidance counselor, or librarian. These people know where to find help. Sometimes a family friend can help. Teens who are religious can often turn to a leader at their place of worship for advice and counseling. Teens can also go to the doctor for a checkup or minor illness and then tell her what's going on. People who are thinking of killing or harming themselves can call the suicide hotline: 1-800-273-TALK (8255). Trained, caring people are there to help, 24-7. The important thing is to reach out for help.

Another thing that keeps people from asking for help is stigma. There are a lot of false ideas out there about depression. Some people still think that depression is a lack of character. Even people who have depression sometimes buy into the stigma. They often blame themselves for being ill. They wouldn't give themselves a hard time for having the flu. But they somehow think that having depression is their fault. It's not.

Cutting and Other Self-Harm

Teens who are depressed sometimes cut themselves. They make small cuts on their bodies, usually their arms and legs. They use razor blades, or knives, or sometimes scissors. Cutters usually aren't trying to kill themselves. The cuts aren't typically very deep. But cutting is a way of harming one's own body. Not all people who cut have depression. They may have other mental illnesses that cause them to want to harm themselves. But cutting can be a problem for people with depression.

It can be hard to understand why a person would cut himself or herself. He or she isn't doing it for attention or as a "cry for help." That's clear because most cutters choose places that can be covered by clothing. They often go to some lengths to hide the cuts from family and friends. Most people do it as a way to interrupt or short-circuit overwhelming emotions. Sometimes people describe feeling overwhelmed as making them want to pull their hair out or bang their heads against a wall. Cutting is equivalent to that but acted on. (And in fact, some troubled teens do bang their heads and pull their hair.) It's not so much that cutters want to injure themselves, as that they need to do something dramatic and painful to distract from their raging emotions. Sometimes depressed people cut for the same reasons that they escalate arguments. It makes them feel something other than the emotional numbness that often accompanies depression.

Cutting is a sign that a person needs help. It may be depression; it may be something else. But it's almost certainly something that can be treated by mental health professionals.

Ongoing Care

Depression requires treatment by mental health professionals. There is, however, a lot people can do to reduce the risk that they'll get depression. And there are things to do to keep depression from getting worse. The first thing, of course, is to get help. That's something that can't be said too many times. Medications for depression can be lifesavers—literally. People with depression should always take their medicines exactly as their doctors tell them to. If they have any side effects, including suicidal thoughts, they should tell their doctor immediately. And if they have suicidal thoughts and can't get in touch with their doctor immediately, they should go to a local emergency room or call 1-800-273-TALK (8255). It's also important to cooperate with therapists and counselors. Mental health professionals can only help if their patients are open and honest with them.

The causes of depression aren't clear. That makes it hard to know how to prevent it. However, there are some things that have been shown to reduce the risk of getting depression. And some things that can

Physicians are happy to talk with patients about their symptoms. They can help discover if the problem is depression or not. They can also start treatment before the illness gets worse.

help people get through an episode of depression and maintain good mental health afterward.

- Eat a healthful diet without too much junk food.
- Get enough sleep.
- Get plenty of exercise.

- Build a good support network of friends and family.
- Don't smoke, drink alcohol, or take any drugs that aren't prescribed by your doctor.
- See your doctor regularly and let her know what's going on in your mind as well as in your body.
- Try to reduce stress in your life as much as you can.
- Get outside—every day if you can.

The key to coping with depression is to recognize it and get help for it.

CHAPTER FIVE

A Little Help from Friends

Not everyone gets depression. But you may have to confront the problem in friends and loved ones. Dealing with your own depression can be difficult. Helping friends and loved ones through it can be challenging, too.

I'm Here

If a friend has a cold, you offer cough drops and comic books. You make hot tea. If you happen to be a good cook, you make chicken soup. But figuring out what to do when a friend has depression is not so easy. In fact, it can be awkward and somctimes even frightening to be around someone who is depressed. However, being around is often the best thing friends can do. Simply letting the person

Sometimes just showing a little support, giving a hug, or offering to listen can be a huge help to people who are struggling.

with depression know he or she is not alone and that he or she has friends who care can be a wonderful thing.

Of course, friends want to do more than that. They want to help! And they can. One of the very first things friends should do is learn as much as they can about depression. This will have two results. First, it will keep them from accidentally buying into dangerous myths and stereotypes. Someone who has done her homework on depression will *not* tell her depressed friend that he just needs to shake it off and get on with life. The second result of learning about this illness is that it prepares friends for what to expect.

Often people expect a friend with depression to be sad. They are patient with that. Sometimes, however, people with depression say hurtful things or behave in strange or disturbing ways. This can be very hard on their friends. When their friend gets angry or lashes out, they don't know how to respond. When she is distracted or keeps missing appointments or breaking promises, her friends may not realize that this behavior is a part of her illness. Sometimes a depressed person can seem like he or she has turned into somebody else. Knowing a little bit about depression can keep these things from being total surprises when they happen. It also helps friends respond with compassion rather than anger.

Probably the next best thing friends can do is listen. That sounds easy, but it's actually a high-level friendship skill. In fact, it's a friendship superpower. Few people really know how to listen. Usually when someone is talking, we want to respond. We're especially eager to get a word in if we think the person needs help. We might even be thinking of what we're going to say to that person while he or she is talking to us. We might be preparing our advice instead of listening. Superhero listeners don't do this. They just listen. They genuinely pay attention to what's being said. Superhero listeners don't judge or try to fix things, either. They just listen.

Sometimes people with depression don't feel like talking. That doesn't mean their friends have to fill the space with chatter. Sitting quietly or going for a quiet walk can often be a big help. When friends do talk to a potentially depressed person, though, there are a few helpful things they can say. First, they need to reassure the person with depression that it's not his or her fault he or she is depressed. People with

People don't have to don capes and become superheroes to help their friends and family who have depression. They just need to hold their hands and stay close.

depression need to know that there is no shame in feeling this way. Second, friends of a person with depression need to encourage their friend to get help if he hasn't already. Friends don't have to be nags. That certainly won't help. But they can say something like, "You know, doctors know how to help people who are feeling like you are. They can help you feel better. Have you thought about telling an adult that you've been feeling bad lately?" Friends can suggest adults they know who will be helpful and trustworthy. Teens can be worried about telling an adult how they're feeling. It can sometimes help if a good friend offers to go along for moral support. That also keeps the person with depression from backing out at the last minute.

Ten Warning Signs of Suicide

According to the Centers for Disease Control and Prevention, suicide is the second-leading cause of death in people ages fifteen to nineteen. That's a very alarming statistic. People who are planning to kill themselves often send out signals. Here are ten signs that someone might be thinking of suicide.

- Talking about suicide or threatening it. Even if the person seems to be joking, frequent references to suicide are an indication that a person might be considering it.
- Talking frequently about death and dying.
- Developing an obsession with celebrities, writers, or historical figures who have died by suicide.
- Developing a sudden interest in weapons or other means of suicide.
- Giving away belongings. It's normal to give stuff away, but when someone seems to be cleaning out his or her treasured belongings, that's definitely a sign to be worried.
- Closing down social media sites for no obvious reason.

- Making comments such as "I may not be here next year."
- Making goodbye calls. People considering suicide will often say goodbye to family and friends. It's not always obvious that they're saying goodbye, though. Phrases like "you were always a good friend to me" can be a clue that something might be up.
- Making comments like "Life isn't worth living" or "My family/friends/the world would be better off without me."
- Suddenly improving or becoming calm. When someone has been deeply depressed, making the decision to kill himself or herself can seem like a relief. This can cause him or her to suddenly seem relaxed and calm.

If you suspect someone is considering suicide, don't wait. Alert a trusted adult immediately or call the suicide hotline at 1-800-273-TALK (8255).

When people are depressed, they often want to keep their illness a secret. That can be tricky for their friends. Friends might realize that this person needs more help than they can give. But telling the person's parents or a teacher about concerns about the depressed friend would violate that person's trust. However, when someone's life is at risk, safety is far more important than keeping secrets. If there is any risk of suicide, then it is crucial to get help. If you suspect a friend might be suicidal, tell a trusted adult immediately. If you can't find anyone quickly, you can call 1-800-273-TALK (8255) for advice about what to do. Sometimes breaking a confidence is better than keeping it. Having a suicidal friend is one of those times.

It's important to be there for people suffering from depression. It's also important for their friends and family to take care of themselves, too. Depression affects everyone it comes near. Friends and family of people with depression should be sure to eat well and get plenty of rest and exercise. They also need to get away from time to time. Spending time with people who aren't depressed can be a great way to recharge. Self-care is essential for people who have friends or family members with depression. It can seem selfish to take care of yourself when someone you know is ill. But friends can't be much help if they aren't healthy. It's important, too, for friends and family to have someone *they* can talk to. Everyone needs support.

Even the happiest families sometimes struggle. There is no shame in having a family member with depression.

Depression Hits Home

Teens aren't the only ones who get depressed. Parents do, too. When a parent is depressed, the illness affects the entire family. It is even more troubling to have a depressed parent than to have a depressed friend. In addition to all the worry and concern, kids' lives just don't go on as usual when a parent suffers from depression. Teens with depressed parents can help

When one person has depression, it can affect the entire family. But by talking about it, with relatives or outside adults like counselors, everyone can heal.

in many of the same ways they help their friends. However, when it's a parent who's depressed, the children need support, too. Kids should not take on all the responsibility themselves if a parent is ill. Other family members are often willing to help if they are asked. It's important for children to reach out for help if they need it. Just as there are resources for people with depression, there are resources for families of people with depression. A family doctor or school guidance counselor can help teens find help coping when a parent is ill.

Oddly, the stigma and shame so often associated with mental illness can be even worse when the ill person is one's parent. We expect our parents to be always healthy—or at least hope they will be. But parents are people, too. They struggle sometimes, just like everyone else. They get sick. There is nothing shameful about having a parent with depression. It isn't his or her fault. And it isn't the fault of the kids. When a parent is depressed, kids might get the idea that their misbehavior, bad grades, surly attitudes, or any number of things caused this problem. That's simply not true. Depression is a biochemical illness. Parents don't get depression because their kids misbehave.

Parents, like many people, often want to keep their problems private. That's understandable. However, if a child suspects that his parent is suicidal, calling for help is not an option. It is imperative. If the parent refuses to get help and there is no other trusted adult to turn to, the child can call the suicide hotline for advice. That number is 1-800-273-TALK (8255). The important thing is to act quickly.

When the Worst Happens

It is very difficult when a friend dies. It can be even more difficult when a friend dies by suicide. The friends and family of suicide victims—the survivors—often feel a great deal of guilt. They ask themselves if there was more they could have done to prevent the tragedy. They wonder why they didn't see it coming. They might continually replay the events of the last time they saw their friend. Was there something, anything, they did wrong or failed to do right?

It's also common for survivors to become very angry with the person who killed themselves. After all, the person is dead. It's the survivors who now have to deal with the pain and loss. They might think "why did you do this to *me*?" Or they may even feel like the suicide was meant as a way of punishing them for not being a good enough friend.

These thoughts and feelings are perfectly normal. However, they are also destructive. It helps if survivors keep in mind that there was nothing they could have done to prevent the suicide. In the end, though we do all we can to help, we can't always save other people.

It is important for survivors to take care of themselves and others. Support groups for friends and family of suicide victims can offer a great deal of help. It might also be helpful for survivors to have psychotherapy. Family doctors and school counselors can recommend where to find this help.

Caution, Teenage Brain Ahead

In her book *The Teenage Brain* neuroscientist Frances E. Jensen explains that adolescents are more impulsive and more likely to take risks than younger children or adults. And according to recent research, teens with depression are even *more* likely to take risks. This is a part of their illness. A study published in 2017 in the *International Journal of Adolescent Medicine and Health* found that depression significantly predicts the occurrence of risky behavior in adolescents. This means that friends of people with depression need to be especially careful.

Driving dangerously or while under the influence of drugs or alcohol are classic risky behaviors of teens. But there are plenty more: smoking or using other tobacco products, using or buying illegal drugs, using firearms, committing vandalism, sexting, having unprotected sex, fighting. The list goes on. It can be difficult for teens to resist friends who are suggesting risky activities. And friends with depression are even more likely to take risks. Being friends with someone who has depression means being especially alert to potential risks.

10 Great Questions to Ask a Depression Specialist

1. Many people in my family have depression. Does this mean that I will get depression, too?
2. I have heard that most depression medicines aren't really very effective. Is this true?
3. I suspect that my friend has depression, but I'm not sure how to ask. Is there a good way to ask someone if he or she is depressed?

4. My mother has severe depression. It makes life hard at home, but I can't ask for help because she doesn't want anyone to know. Do I have any options?

5. My doctor wants me to go to psychotherapy sessions once a week. I want to give it a try so I can get better, but how do I tell my friends I'm leaving school early to go see a shrink?

6. My friend is obsessed with celebrities who have killed themselves. Does this mean he's thinking of killing himself? What should I do?

7. I like the goth look, but I'm not at all depressed. Yet people seem to think the two things go hand in hand. How can I explain that they don't?

8. My sister killed herself a couple of years ago. Everyone thinks I should be over it by now, but I'm not. What can I do to feel better?

9. My dad is depressed, and I understand that it is an illness. I have more trouble understanding why he's so often angry and mean-spirited. Is this a part of his depression?

10. I'm worried about my little brother. I know teens can get depression, but can little kids get it, too?

CHAPTER SIX

Better Times Ahead

People may have always suffered from depression, but that doesn't mean the illness has always been well understood. Over the years, people have had many different theories about causes and approaches to treatment. It is only recently that science and society have begun to crack open the mysteries of this all-too-common illness. And that has led not only to better medical treatments, but to better attitudes about depression.

From Demons to Druggists

Hippocrates, the father of medicine, did indeed recognize depression—what he called melancholia.

He realized that it was an illness. This was a great improvement on previous ideas about depression. Before Hippocrates, most people thought people with depression had been possessed by demons or other evil spirits. The treatment for depression in those days was often exorcism. In many ancient cultures, exorcism did not involve simply saying prayers and ringing bells. People thought to be possessed were likely to be beaten or nearly starved in order to drive out the demons.

Hippocrates had a different theory of what caused depression and much different suggestions for how to treat it. By this time, physicians thought that the body contained four substances they called humors. The humors were blood, phlegm, yellow bile, and black bile. They believed that melancholia was caused by having too much black bile. The cure? Bathing, exercise, and a special diet. And, alas, also bloodletting, which was meant to remove excessive humors from the body.

Medical treatments for patients with depression improved, but slowly. The possession theory made a brief comeback. Sadly, people with depression were often put in mental asylums. Then, during the European Renaissance (the fourteenth, fifteenth, and sixteenth centuries), the idea of bodily humors caught on once again. However, at various times and places in those years, people with mental illnesses were thought to be witches and were often killed. In the early seventeenth century, an English scholar named Robert Burton wrote a remarkable book about depression (among many, many other things). It was called *The Anatomy of Melancholy*. Lots of things make this very long, very strange, and often very funny book remarkable. But worth noting here is that Burton addressed how both physical and social conditions could be at the root of depression. He specifically mentioned poverty.

The eighteenth and nineteenth centuries have been called the age of enlightenment. But people were only slightly enlightened when it came to depression. By this time, physicians had begun to realize that heredity played a role in depression. However, many of them thought that it played the *only* role. They believed the illness was untreatable. Once again, people with depression were often locked away in prisons or madhouses or hidden away in attics and back rooms of their families' homes.

Things improved greatly in the twentieth century. Scientists began to learn more about the anatomy and physiology of the brain. This helped them understand that depression is an illness that can be treated. During the first part of the twentieth century, the favored treatment for depression was psychotherapy (also called talk therapy). Soon, scientists began to better understand the chemical imbalances that contribute to depression. This led to a shift to treatments with drugs. Many useful depression drugs were discovered in the latter part of the twentieth century. These were life changing for many people suffering from depression. By the dawn of the twenty-first century, people had come to understand that depression is caused by a combination of factors. It can't be pinned down to just one chemical or just one experience. Chemical imbalances in the brain, life experiences, and social conditions all play a role in bringing on the illness. Now treatments try to address all of these.

Helping Each Other

As science has refined its understanding of depression, the public has as well. It has taken a while, though. Even today, the public sometimes misunderstands depression. There are still many myths and stereotypes about depression. There is also a lot of stigma remaining. Some people still think that depression is a lack of willpower or a weakness of character. Some people use words like "crazy" or "mad" to describe people with mental illness. However, that is changing rapidly. And young people are helping make that change.

Many organizations, such as the National Alliance on Mental Illness (NAMI), have launched campaigns to educate the public about depression and other mental illnesses and to eliminate the stigma. NAMI also works to influence public policy about mental illness. In addition, NAMI offers a six-week education program for families and caregivers of children and teens with depression.

The Kid Was Not All Right

It can be difficult to talk openly about having depression. Celebrities—who otherwise share so much of their lives with the public—also find it difficult. But when famous people tell their stories, it can be a big help to their fans.

The rapper Scott Mescudi, who uses the stage name Kid Cudi, realized this. When he finally sought help for his long-term depression, he shared that with his fans. He had, he said, been living a lie by pretending to be fine when he was actually struggling with serious depression.

On October 4, 2016, Mescudi posted a notice on his Facebook page. He told his fans that he had long suffered from terrible depression and was near suicide. He announced that he had checked himself into a facility for treatment for depression and suicidal thoughts. He wrote, "I am not at peace. I haven't been since you've known me. If I didn't come here, I would've done something to myself."

(continued on the next page)

(continued from the previous page)

A few weeks later, he emerged a changed man. In a July 19, 2018, interview with *Billboard* magazine, Mescudi told Hanif Abdurraqib, "I'm the best I've ever been in my life. I realized I was genuinely happy…to be still doing what I love. Taking care of my responsibilities, and my daughter's good and my family's good. Creating is making me happy again."

Mescudi sought help for his depression. More than that, he spoke openly about his struggles with mental illness because, as he told Abdurraqib, "I needed to be honest with the kids."

Education and awareness programs can also help prevent depression. In 2009, the University of Michigan teamed up with Ann Arbor, Michigan, public schools to launch a program called Peer-to-Peer Depression Awareness Campaign, P2P for short. The goals were to educate high school students about depression and to help them find creative ways to share this knowledge with their friends and

Rapper Kid Cudi performs at Lollapalooza Chicago 2015. His fans did not then know that at the time he was struggling with severe depression.

classmates. It was hoped that this would encourage teens with depression to seek help as well as reduce the stigma surrounding depression.

In March 2018, the researchers reported on the success of the P2P program in a paper published in the medical journal *Psychiatric Services*. The study found that after P2P, students were more likely to feel confident identifying symptoms of depression in themselves and others. They were willing to ask for help from teachers, coaches, clergy members, or a helpline if they experienced those symptoms for two weeks or more. They felt comfortable discussing mental health with friends and at school. They said they would not be embarrassed to be seen visiting a social worker or psychiatrist. In addition, they said they knew that depression could not be controlled by willpower.

One of the cool things about the P2P program is that students got to decide what methods they want to use to educate their peers. After training sessions, students themselves create resources, including videos, printed material, assemblies, posters, and confidential helplines.

Meanwhile, Back in the Lab

While the public has been improving its attitudes about mental illness, scientists have been busy, too. A deeper understanding of the biology of the disease

Many types of programs, like remote talk therapy, are now available to help people understand their depression and seek help for themselves or their families.

is creating hope for exciting new therapies. Until recently, most research into the biochemical causes of depression focused on neurotransmitters, like serotonin. However, in the last few years researchers have been looking even deeper—at the level of brain cells. Mitochondria are parts of cells that produce

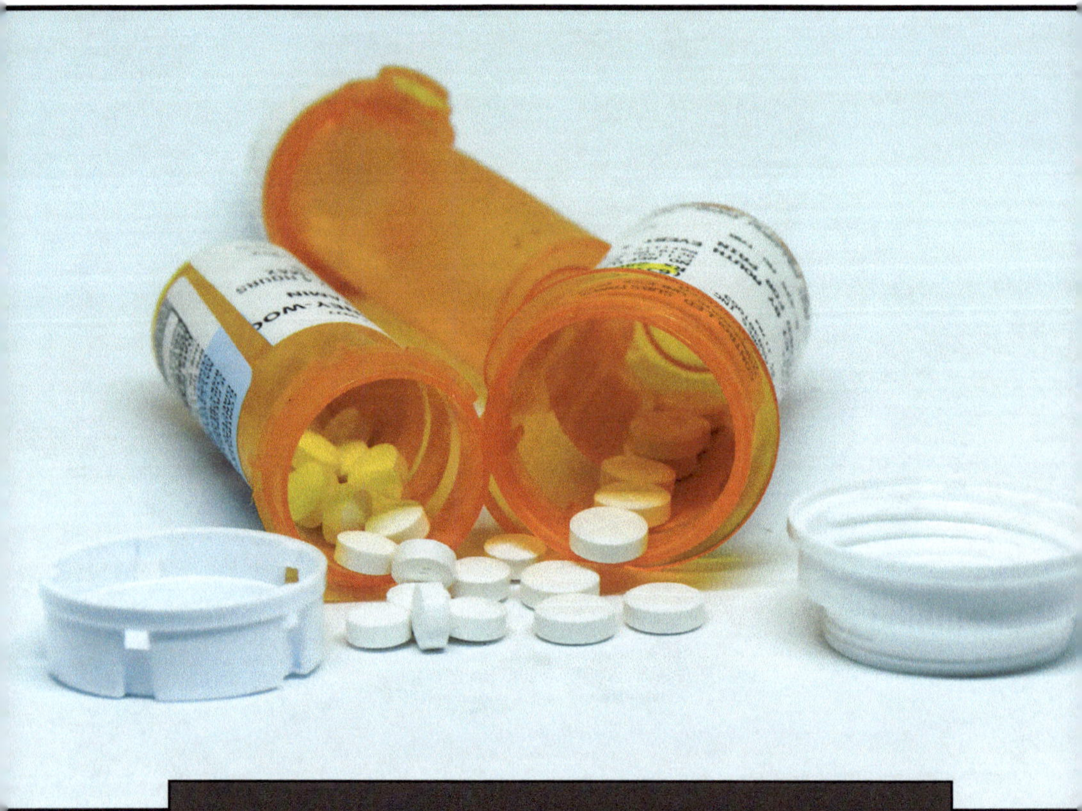

Self-medicating is a bad idea. But taking the medicines a doctor prescribes—exactly as he or she prescribes them—can be an enormous help to people with depression.

energy for the cell. Some researchers now think that when mitochondria do not function properly, it can start a long chain of events that eventually causes depression. They are working on drugs that make mitochondria function properly.

Some drugs currently used for other illnesses are being studied because they seem to be able to quickly reverse suicidal thoughts. A drug used to treat amyotrophic lateral sclerosis (ALS), also known as Lou Gehrig's disease, has also shown some promise in treating depression.

Depression research is not limited to drugs. Some physicians are treating depression with a new technique called TMS. TMS stands for transcranial magnetic stimulation. It is not yet approved for use in children and adolescents, but may one day be available for young people, too. TMS aims magnetic pulses at the part of the brain that regulates mood. Researchers aren't sure exactly how this works. However, they think that it stimulates parts of the brain that become less active during depression.

All of these treatments are either new or still on the horizon. No doubt there will be more exciting developments in the coming years.

Other therapies that aren't new but are unconventional are getting renewed attention in depression treatment. Hypnosis, meditation, and even laughter therapy are being taken seriously. They seem to be effective in many patients.

Of course, psychotherapy is still one of the best treatments for depression. Surprisingly, certain types of psychotherapy have been shown to actually

Thanks to today's treatments and better social understanding of mental illness, people with depression can look forward to a happier future.

make changes in the brain. A study published in January 2017 in the medical journal *Translational Psychiatry* discovered some interesting things about cognitive behavioral therapy (CBT). The brains of people who had had CBT had more connections between different regions of their brains after therapy than before. The more connections they developed, the more effective the treatment was. This study, and others like it, have given support to people who say that psychotherapy is a good treatment for depression.

The world has come a long way since people believed depression was caused by demons and best treated with cruelty. And it has come a long way since people thought depression was a weakness of will or a character flaw. Now that we see depression for what it is—a serious yet treatable illness—there is an enormous amount of hope for people with depression and their friends and families.

Glossary

adolescence The time of life immediately surrounding puberty, when a young person becomes physically adult.

anatomy The study of the structure of the bodies of humans and other living things.

angst A feeling of anxiety, dread, or insecurity.

bile A bitter substance secreted by the liver and stored in the gallbladder; one of the four bodily humors of ancient medicine.

biochemical Having to do with the chemical processes of humans and other living things.

clergy People who are officially ordained to perform religious ceremonies and other duties, especially in Christian churches.

CT scan Short for computed tomography scan, a diagnostic test used to look at internal tissues, such as organs and bones.

curate To carefully select and assemble material to give a certain impression or information.

debilitating Describing a situation or illness that is so severe that it makes a person unable to function normally.

deduce To reach a conclusion using logical reasoning.

hormone A substance produced by an organism that stimulates cells or tissues to act in certain ways.

madhouse Historically, a name for a mental institution or psychiatric hospital.

manic Exhibiting an unusual, often pathological, amount of energy and excitement.

melancholy A feeling or attitude of extreme sadness.

neuroscientist A scientist who specializes in the study of the brain and nervous system.

peer A person in the same social group or age bracket.

perfectionism An unreasonable desire or expectation that everything be exactly right.

pessimism A tendency to look at the negative side of things.

phlegm A thick substance secreted by the mucous membranes; one of the four bodily humors of ancient medicine.

physiology The study of the functions of the parts of humans and other living things.

receptor A cell that can receive chemical instructions and transmit instructions to a nerve cell.

sadism Deriving pleasure from inflicting humiliation or pain on other people.

screen To test for indicators of a particular disease or condition.

stereotype A fixed and often superficial or erroneous image of or opinion about a person or thing.

stigma A mark of shame or disgrace associated with something or someone.

For More Information

Canadian Mental Health Association (CMHA)
250 Dundas Street West, Suite 500
Toronto, ON M5T 2Z5
(416) 646-5557
Email: info@cmha.ca
Website: http://www.cmha.ca
Facebook: @CMHA.ACSM.National
Instagram: @cmhanational
Twitter: @CMHA_NTL
CMHA helps people in communities all across Canada get access to the resources they need to maintain and improve their mental health.

Families for Depression Awareness
391 Totten Pond Road, Suite 101
Waltham, MA 02451
(781) 890-0220
Email: info@familyaware.org
Website: http://www.familyaware.org
Facebook and Twitter: @familyaware
Families for Depression Awareness is an organization that offers a variety of support services, including education and training, to help families cope with depression and other mood disorders.

Mental Health America (MHA)
500 Montgomery Street, Suite 820
Alexandria, VA 22314
(703) 684-7722
(800) 969-6642
Website: http://www.mentalhealthamerica.net
Facebook and Instagram: @mentalhealthamerica
Twitter: @mentalhealtham
MHA is a community-based organization that offers support services, including prevention, to Americans of all ages living with mental illness.

National Alliance on Mental Illness (NAMI)
3803 N. Fairfax Drive, Suite 100
Arlington, VA 22203
(800) 950-6264
Email: info@nami.org
Website: http://www.nami.org
Facebook: @NAMI
Instagram: @NAMICommunicate
Twitter: @namicommunicate
NAMI is a grassroots mental health organization that works to educate the public and influence government and social policy related to the care and treatment of people with mental illness.

Suicide Prevention Lifeline
Website: http://www.suicidepreventionlifeline.org/help-yourself/youth
Facebook: @800273talk
Twitter and YouTube: @800273TALK
In addition to providing emergency crisis counseling, the Suicide Prevention Lifeline supports a variety of initiatives to improve crisis services and advance suicide prevention.

Teen Line
Cedars-Sinai
PO Box 48750
Los Angeles, CA 90048-0750
(310) 855-HOPE (4673)
(800) TLC-TEEN (852-8336) (U.S. & Canada only)
Website: https://teenlineonline.org
Facebook and Instagram: @teenlineonline
Twitter: @TEENLINEONLINE
Teen Line is an organization that uses a helpline and modern communication technologies to help troubled teens address their problems before they become a crisis.

Youth Mental Health Canada (YMHC)
(416) 915-3542
Email: admin@youthmentalhealth.ca
Website: https://ymhc.ngo
Facebook: @YMHECanada
Instagram: @youth_mental_health
Twitter: @YMHEActionGroup
YMHC is youth driven and youth led. The organization focuses on education and advocacy, working for public funding for culturally sensitive, needs-based services.

For Further Reading

Cobain, Bev. *When Nothing Matters Anymore: A Survival Guide for Depressed Teens.* Minneapolis, MN: Free Spirit, 2007.

Ford, Michael Thomas. *Suicide Notes*. New York, NY: Harper Collins, 2008.

Green, John. *Looking for Alaska*. New York, NY: Dutton, 2005.

Jensen, Kelly, ed. *Don't Call Me Crazy: 33 Voices Start the Conversation About Mental Health.* New York, NY: Algonquin Young Readers, 2018.

Landau, Jennifer. *Teens Talk About Anxiety and Depression*. New York, NY: Rosen, 2018.

Marsico, Kate. *Depression and Stress*. New York, NY: Cavendish Square, 2014.

McCormick, Patricia. *Cut*. New York, NY: Push, 2000.

Parks, Peggy J. *Teen Depression*. Detroit, MI: Lucent, 2013.

Sedley, Ben. *Stuff That Sucks: A Teen's Guide to Accepting What You Can't Change and Committing to What You Can*. Oakland, CA: Instant Help Books, 2017.

Toner, Jacqueline B., and Claire A. B. Freeland. *Depression: A Teen's Guide to Survive and Thrive*. Washington, DC: Magination Press (The American Psychological Association), 2016.

Bibliography

Abdurraqib, Hanif. "How Kid Cudi Found Joy After Fighting Depression: 'I'm the Best I've Ever Been,." *Billboard*, July 19, 2018. https://www.billboard.com/articles/columns/hip-hop/8466037/kid-cudi-interview-billboard-cover-story-2018.

Anderson, Jenny. "Even Teens Are Worried They Spend Too Much Time on Their Phones." *Quartz*, August 23, 2018. https://qz.com/1367506/pew-research-teens-worried-they-spend-too-much-time-on-phones.

BlueCross BlueShield. "Major Depression: The Impact on Overall Health." May 10, 2018. https://www.bcbs.com/the-health-of-america/reports/major-depression-the-impact-overall-health.

Bratman, Gregory N., et al. "Nature Experience Reduces Rumination and Subgenual Prefrontal Cortex Activation." *Proceedings of the National Academy of Sciences*, June 29, 2015. https://doi.org/10.1073/pnas.1510459112.

Burton, Robert. *The Anatomy of Melancholy*, originally published in 1621. Adelaide, South Australia: University of Adelaide, 2014. https://

ebooks.adelaide.edu.au/b/burton/robert/melancholy/index.html.

Centers for Disease Control and Prevention. National Center for Health Statistics. "Adolescent Health." Retrieved October 30, 2018. https://www.cdc.gov/nchs/fastats/adolescent-health.htm.

Cuffe, Steven P. "Do Antidepressants Increase the Risk of Suicide in Children and Adolescents?" American Academy of Child and Adolescent Psychiatry. Retrieved November 5, 2018. https://www.aacap.org/aacap/medical_students_and_residents/mentorship_matters/developmentor/Do_Antidepressants_Increase_the_Risk_of_Suicide_in_Children_and_Adolescents.aspx.

Davidson, Jonathan R. T., et al. "Mental Illness In U.S. Presidents Between 1776 and 1974: A Review of Biographical Sources." *The Journal of Nervous and Mental Disease*, January 2006. https://insights.ovid.com/crossref?an=00005053-200601000-00009.

Ghaemi, Nassir. *A First-Rate Madness: Uncovering the Links Between Leadership and Mental Illness.* New York, NY: Penguin, 2011.

Harvard Health. "What Causes Depression?"

Retrieved October 30, 2018. https://www.health.harvard.edu/mind-and-mood/what-causes-depression.

Haynes, Trevor. "Dopamine, Smartphones, and You: A Battle for your Time." *Science in the News*, Harvard University Graduate School of Arts and Sciences, May 1, 2018. http://sitn.hms.harvard.edu/flash/2018/dopamine-smartphones-battle-time.

Horwitz, Allan, et al. "History of Depression." In *Oxford Handbook of Mood Disorders*, edited by Robert J. DeRubeis and Daniel R. Strunk, 11–23. Oxford, UK: Oxford University Press, 2017.

Jaing, Jingjing. "How Teens and Parents Navigate Screen Time and Device Distractions." Pew Research Center, August 22, 2018. http://www.pewinternet.org/2018/08/22/how-teens-and-parents-navigate-screen-time-and-device-distractions.

Jensen, Frances E., with Amy Ellis Nutt. *The Teenage Brain: A Neuroscientist's Survival Guide to Raising Adolescents and Young Adults*. New York, NY: Harper, 2015.

Levine, Bruce. "How Seven Historic Figures

Overcame Depression Without Doctors." *Counterpunch*, November 30, 2012. https://www.counterpunch.org/2012/11/30/how-7-historic-figures-overcame-depression-without-doctors.

Mason, Liam, et al. "Brain Connectivity Changes Occurring Following Cognitive Behavioural Therapy for Psychosis Predict Long-Term Recovery." *Translational Psychiatry*, January 17, 2017. https://www.nature.com/articles/tp2016263.

National Alliance on Mental Health. "Mental Health by the Numbers." Retrieved November 5, 2018. https://www.nami.org/Learn-More/Mental-Health-By-the-Numbers.

National Institute of Mental Health. "Prevalence of Major Depressive Episodes Among Adolescents." Depression. Retrieved November 5, 2018. https://www.nimh.nih.gov/health/statistics/major-depression.shtml#part_155031.

National Institute of Mental Health. "Suicide Prevention." Retrieved November 5, 2018. https://www.nimh.nih.gov/health/topics/suicide-prevention/index.shtml.

O'Connor, Briannon C., et al. "Usual Care for

Adolescent Depression from Symptom Identification Through Treatment Initiation," *JAMA Pediatrics* 170, no. 4 (2016): 373–380.

Parikh, Sagar V., et al. "The Michigan Peer-to-Peer Depression Awareness Program: School-Based Prevention to Address Depression Among Teens." *Psychiatric Services*, March 1, 2018. https://ps.psychiatryonline.org/doi/10.1176/appi.ps.201700101.

Schrobsdorff, Susanna. "Teen Depression and Anxiety: Why the Kids Are Not Alright." *Time*, October 27, 2016. http://time.com/4547322/american-teens-anxious-depressed-overwhelmed.

Schrobsdorff, Susanna. "There's a Startling Increase of Major Depression Among Teens in the US." *Time*, November 16, 2016. http://time.com/4572593/increase-depression-teens-teenage-mental-health.

Soleimani, M. A. "The Relationship Between Anxiety, Depression and Risk Behaviors in Adolescents." *International Journal of Adolescent Medicine and Health*, May 11, 2017. https://www.ncbi.nlm.nih.gov/pubmed/28493817.

Statistics Canada. "Leading Causes of Death, Total Population, By Age Group." Retrieved

November 5, 2018. https://www150.statcan.gc.ca/t1/tbl1/en/tv.action?pid=1310039401.

Sugarman, Joe. "The Rise of Teen Depression." *John Hopkins Health Review*, Fall/Winter 2017. https://www.johnshopkinshealthreview.com/issues/fall-winter-2017/articles/the-rise-of-teen-depression.

Treneman, Ann. "J. K. Rowling, the Interview." *Times of London*, June 30, 2000. http://www.accio-quote.org/articles/2000/0600-times-treneman.html.

Wallace, David Foster. "The Depressed Person." *Harper's*, January, 1998.

Weissman, Myrna M., et al. "A 30-Year Study of Three Generations at High Risk and Low Risk for Depression." *JAMA Psychiatry*, August 10, 2016. https://jamanetwork.com/journals/jamapsychiatry/fullarticle/2542680.

Zuckerbrot, Rachel A., et al. "Guidelines for Adolescent Depression in Primary Care (GLAD-PC): Part I. Practice Preparation, Identification, Assessment, and Initial Management." *Pediatrics*, March 2018. http://pediatrics.aappublications.org/content/141/3/e20174081.

Index

T

W

About the Author

Avery Elizabeth Hurt is the author of many books for children and young adults. In her days as a science and medical journalist, she often researched and wrote about issues related to mental illness, particularly depression.

Photo Credits

Cover Andrii Kobryn/Shutterstock.com; p. 5 dboystudio/Shutterstock.com; p. 6 StasyKID/Shutterstock.com; p. 7 Monkey Business Images/Shutterstock.com; p. 9 Dusan Milenkovic/Shutterstock.com; p. 13 Alys Tomlinson/Cultura/Getty Images; p. 17 (left) H. Armstrong Roberts/ClassicStock/Archive Photos/Getty Images, (right) Carl Mydans/The LIFE Picture Collection/Getty Images; p. 19 Walter McBride/WireImage/Getty Images; p. 23 Photo 12/Universal Images Group/Getty Images; p. 26 Ryan McVay/Photodisc/Getty Images; p. 31 Kateryna Kon/Shutterstock.com; p. 36 National Suicide Prevention Lifeline; p. 38 Hero Images/Getty Images; p. 41 Marco Piunti/E+/Getty Images; p. 46 karen roach/Shutterstock.com; p. 48 AnemStyle/Shutterstock.com; p. 52 Alexander Image/Shutterstock.com; p. 57 izusek/E+/Getty Images; p. 63 adamkaz/E+/Getty Images; p. 66 gawrav/E+/Getty Images; p. 69 ER Productions Limited/DigitalVision/Getty Images; p. 73 © iStockphoto.com/Multiart; p. 74 aldomurillo/E+/Getty Images; p. 87 Michael Hickey/Getty Images; p. 89 InkkStudios/iStock/Getty Images; p. 90 WoodysPhotos/Shutterstock.com; p. 92 Maskot/Getty Images.

Design and Layout: Nicole Russo-Duca; Editor: Elissa Petruzzi; Photo Researcher: Sherri Jackson